Mexican Slang A Guide

by Linton H. Robinson

First edition, 1992
    second printing 1994

Bueno Books
    a division of In One EAR Publications
    29481 Manzanita Drive
    Campo CA 91906-1128
    ©1992, 1994 by In One EAR Publications

Library of Congress Cataloging in Publication Data

Robinson, Linton H., 1948-
    Mexican slang / by Linton H. Robinson.—1st ed. p. cm.
    Spanish phrases with English translation, elaboration.
    ISBN 0-9627080-7-0 : $6.95
    1. Spanish language—Slang. 2. Regionalisms I. Title

    Printed in the U.S.A.
    ISBN 0-9627080-7-0

Table of Contents

SLEAZY MORAL DISCLAIMER

It will be quickly noticed that this lexicon contains a wide range of slang terms, including the vulgar and even obscene. This was the result of a decision we made only after much soul-searching, moral discussion, and sniggering. We decided it would be pointless to omit phrases that are commonly heard. We are not advocating that readers run around foreign countries spewing nasty words, (and of course if you are offended by coarse language, read no further and all that) but it is helpful to know what is meant by words that one hears—and to know what words to avoid repeating.

To that end we have tried to categorize questionable words by the kind of company in which they are acceptable. "Polite" means acceptable in any company, "acceptable" means in mixed company of professional adults. (Our standard is the younger crowd in the Tijuana Bicultural League; let's say a JayCee's meeting.)

Aside from terms here that may be vulgar, crude, or downright nasty, there are others which, while acceptable, may have street connotations that would sound like "gutter talk" in polite company. Others are youth slang and as such can make your speech sound hip to some or silly and juvenile to others. It is not a bad idea to follow the example of your company when using vulgar or street terms, and to ask someone privately when in doubt. If you commit a *faux pas*, it never hurts to include in your apology a reminder that you are not a native speaker.

Keep in mind that words change meaning in different countries. To call a man **cabrón**, for instance, is common and relatively tame in Mexico, but in Cuba and some other countries means that you have cuckolded him, and is a grave insult capable of turning a friend into an enemy instantly. It is best to be careful of insults at first, even playful ones. In Brazil, by the way, **cabrón** means "handsome" or "foxy."

THE OBLIGATORY BORING SCHOLARLY INTRODUCTION

It would be impossible to discuss Spanish slang in totality, since there is different slang in every country and region. Mexico alone has a rich and multi-leveled idiomatic vocabulary of thousands of words, and many terms that are used colloquially in Chiapas are never heard in Veracruz. Furthermore, there are Dantesque levels of societal usage, some obscure or unknown even to Mexicans. However, our concern here is not esoteric folklore, but "standard" Mexican slang, words that are widely heard or read in comic books, TV shows, and rock records.

Within the wide and varied tapestry of Mexican slang are several main strains worth mention, specific examples of which are included later in the text:

La onda came out of 1960's hippie cant, but is still current and **¿Qué onda?** is a very common greeting among the young and hip. **Onda** means wave (as in microwave) or vibrations. **Buena onda** means, essentially "good vibes." **Ondas** are expressions, folkways, or manners. "YouthSpeak" would be **Ondas Adolescentes**, Mexican jokes and slang such as those in the this book would be **ondas mexicanas**.

Caló (a word which originally referred to the cant of Spanish gypsies) or **calichi** is underground, criminal argot, particularly from the poor barrios of Mexico City—pure gutter talk. As impenetrable as the similar Cockney slang, **caló** mutates as fast as ghetto rap or surfer lingo and there is always some new twist for the explorer.

"Spanglish" border talk, is also called **fronterazos** or **pochismos** after **pochos**, or Mexicans who live on the U. S. side of the border. Viewed by the academy as a degeneration of Spanish if not a form of linguistic imperialism, border usage is mercurial and often very funny. There are several ways in which English and Spanish meld: A Spanish word like **educación** which technically means "upbringing" starts being used to mean "education" due to imitation of American usage.

English words are also "Spanglishized," as in **huacha** meaning "watch" or **bloque** to mean a cement block. Transliterations such as **"Dame quebrada"** for "Gimme a break" (even though **quebrar** means "break" only in the sense of "broken") give the **jerga fronteriza** (border jargon) a sort of pun structure transparent to the completely bilingual but mystifying to others. We include a tiny fraction of this burgeoning vocabulary in this book but make no attempt at a comprehensive collection since it is not useful to travellers, fades off into

Spanish and English slang so subtly, and changes too fast to nail down.

LINGUISTIC and
PRONUNCIATION NOTES

We assume that readers already have a basic command of Spanish. If not, get one before you run around spouting slang. The publishers of *The Guide To Mexican Slang* produce several books for learning basic Spanish. Ordering **dos chelas** instead of **dos cervezas** is no big deal, and can give you the panache for which you probably purchased this book, but speaking more slang than Spanish will only make you look like an idiot.

Likewise, we assume you are familiar with Spanish pronunciation and are aware of gender endings. (If guys are **chavos**, chicks are **chavas**, if a bald man is **pelón** a bald woman is a **pelona**, old men are **viejitos**, old women **viejitas**, etc.) We also assume you can conjugate Spanish verbs, which are presented here in the infinitive form. (If not, just use the infinitives—you'll sound primitive, but will be understood.)

As far as pronunciation, remember that "ñ" is pronounced as "ny" in "canyon," "ll" is pronounced as "y." "J" is always pronounced as "h;" "h" is always silent, an initial "g" is pronounced as "h," unless followed by "u," in which case the diphthong is pronounced almost like "w." If a word ends in "l" or "r" it is accented on the last syllable. All other words are accented on the second to last syllable unless another syllable bears an accent mark. Vowels are simple, pure, and always pronounced the same:

a—as in "ah" or "mama"

e—like the long "a" in "make" or "way"

i—like the long "e" in "feel" or "see"

o—as in "old" or "no"

u—without the initial "y" sound, as in "kudos" or "rude".

I. TRANSLATED AMERICANISMS

The Labyrinth of "Golly, Dude!"

COOL: A major expression with many synonyms in both tongues.

Padre

Is the most direct equivalent, as in "He's a really cool singer," **Es cantante muy padre**. Can be used impersonally, like "Far out!" **¡Ay, que padre!** Extremely cool would be **padrsimo**.

Curado

Similar to **padre** but hipper. Probably comes from the pun of **padre** meaning **cura** (priest).

Suave

While it means "smooth" or "soft," **suave** also has a definite equivalence to "cool" and **suavecito** is cooler yet. The Camel Filter "cool character" billboards in Mexico say **Un Tipo Suave**.

Chingón

A tougher, more masculine, street connotation, it could describe a car, motorcycle, or person and might be thought of as meaning "stud." Not polite, but highly visible on T-shirts and caps. **Que coche más chingón** is "What a cool car."

Chido

Means "cool" or "bitchin'" in urban gutter talk, but getting to be a popular term with "yuppies."

Estar de pelos

Hip, youth slang. Something like "rad" or "too much." **La camisa está de pelos** is "The shirt is way cool." A variation is **"pasar de peluche."** **Peluche** is fleece and **un osito de peluche** is a teddy bear. The very latest "Youthspeak" as we go to press is **de pelos y jícamas**.

Simpático

Means "nice," especially of people. Nice people are also **bonito, lindo, buena onda. Él es gran tipo** means "He's a great guy." You could also say, **¡Que tipazo!**—"What a guy!"

In fact, the use of the **-azo** ending, which implies a blow with or explosion of the word modified, is good for homemade slang. We recently heard a woman summon a good looking young waiter by calling, **"Jovenazo,"** and a guy talking about greeting his girlfriend back from a long trip with a **colchonazo** (mattress attack).

Impersonally, **bonito** is literally the diminutive of "good," and means "nice." **Que bonito** is "How nice."

Caer Bien

To be **simpático**. **Él me cae bien** is the way to say such things as, "I like him," "He's all right," "He's cool with me." Better usage than **me gusta** when discussing people—especially people of the same sex.

Prendido

Prender means to turn on a light or light a fire, so something **muy prendido** is a real turn-on. **Me prende** means "it turns me on."

Bárbara

Means "barbaric," but as an exclamation means, "Way cool," "Far Out," etc. But **Que barbaridad** (which comes from the same root) means, "What a bummer" or "Disgraceful." Additionally, **una barbaridad de** means "a lot of," yet **cuesta una barbaridad** means "it costs an arm and a leg." Go figure.

Tranquilo

Means calm or serene, but is also "cool" in the sense of "cool it," "chill out," or calm down. Can be used as a one-word imperative. **Calmada** is similar to **tranquila** and **la cosa es calmada** or **toda calmada** means "everything's cool."

UNCOOL

Feo, Gacho

Feo means ugly, but is used in many deprecative senses, road conditions, weather, behavior, music, can be **feo**, so it could mean, "lousy," "in bad repair," etc. Used impersonally, **feo** has sense of "a drag," "a bummer," "it sucks." Used about a person, it means "ugly," unless applied to certain characteristics: **Tiene carácter feo** means "He's got a rotten character." **Gacho** is street slang and has all the same connotations. Can be used personally or impersonally; ¡**Que gacho!** means "That sucks!" or "Bummer" or "What a drag." **Eres gacho** means "You stink." **No seas gacho** is "Don't be a drag" or "Come off it."

Pesado

Literally means "heavy," but has a negative connotation in slang, very **antipático**. Generally applied to a person. Can mean boring, a drag, a creep. Also **pesadito**.

Other terms include, **sangrón, peseta, caer en los huevos, chocante.** One frequently hears **No seas sangrón,** or **No seas pesado** for "Don't be a pain in the ass."

Chingado

Screwed up, jerked around, or simply fucked as in the T-Shirts that say **Estoy chingado.**

Caer Gordo

Literally, "to fall fat," this is the opposite of **caer bien. Ella me cae gorda** means, "I don't like her," "she's a bummer," "She rubs me the wrong way."

If you want to use an expression which is less slangy try **caer mal**.

Fuchi

Stinky, smelly. But by extension, anything corrupt, perverse, kinky, or not to the liking. As an exclamation, means "Phew!" or "Yuck!" Also **fu** or **furris.**

¡**Wácala!** (also spelled **guácala**) also means "Ugh!" "Yech!" "Gross!" or "Barf!" but is more about taste than smell. The comment is *de rigueur* when spitting something out on the floor.

Asombroso

Though it actually comes from the root **sombra** and literally signifies "overshadowing," it curiously means what it sounds like—"awesome."

FUNNY

Chistoso

From **chiste**—a joke. Means "funny" in the sense of comical, someone who jokes a lot. Other words for "joke" include **broma** (and the verb **bromear**) and **cotorro**. In Spanish, incidentally, there are no "dirty" jokes, but **chistes colorados** for "blue" material and **chistes verdes**, which are "sick" or off-color jokes. **Raspa** is a bad joke or pun (pun is **albur**, the verb **alburear**).

Gracioso

Also funny, as in "Very funny,"—**muy gracioso** or "What's so funny"—**¿Qué tiene de gracioso?** A noun as in **¿Quién fue el gracioso?** (Who's the wise guy?) A humorous person; indicates natural humor more than formal joking.

Vaciado

Slang term, meaning funny in the sense of "a kick" or something that tickles one. "It's a scream that your mom likes rock music," would be **Que vaciado que le gusta el rock a tu mami**.

Not related to **vacilar**, to joke around.

Burlar

To joke or kid around. **Burla** is a joke, prank, or jest. (Differs from **chiste** as telling a joke differs from an April Fool jest).

"You're kidding" is **Me burlas**. "Don't put me on" would be **No te burles**. A joker or "card" would be described as **burlesco**.

Picarón

Picar means to sting, pick, or bite, like a mosquito, but the word has wide application. "Hot" food, for example is **picante**. "Is this **salsa** very hot?" would be **¿Pica mucho?**

There is also the use of **pica** in the sense of a bird's beak, and thus as a sobriquet for the penis. But a major use is in mention of joking and jesting—**picarón** is a joker, a "card," the thing to call someone who's just put one over on you or told a good one. The sense is more towards barbed or racy humor and **picaresco** means exactly that—a song with **letra picaresca** is a racy or sexy one.

Payasear

Fooling around, clowning around, kidding.
Payaso means "clown." "Just kidding" would be
Nomás estoy payaseando. No seas payaso would
mean "Cut the clowning."

Caer el veinte

To "get" a joke can be expressed as **caer el
veinte**, referring to the 20 **centavo** coins used in
telephones, and equivalent to our expression, "the
coin finally dropped." **Por fin le cayó el veinte**
means "He finally got it." **Caer** (to fall) by the way,
is the way of expressing "fall for it." **Caíste** means

"You fell for it" or "Gotcha!" **No cayó** means "He didn't bite."

Tomar los pelos

Literally (taking the hair), this means "pulling my leg." **¿Estás en serio o me estás tomando los pelos?** would mean "Are you serious, or are you pulling my leg?"

Raro

The English use of "funny" to mean "odd" or "peculiar" does not follow in Spanish. "That's odd" would be **curiosa** and "weird" is **raro**. "This soup tastes funny" would be **Esta sopa tiene un gusto raro. Tipos raros** are strange people or weirdos.

FOXY

(All these can be used with **bien** to mean "pretty cute," "really foxy," etc). **Guapo** is handsome, **guapa** is foxy. Both can be used as an address; (**Hola, Guapo** means "Hello, Handsome"); or as a noun (**Hay muchas guapas** would mean "There are a lot of foxes around.) Other adjectives that can be feminized by changing the final "o" to "a" are **lindo, bonito,** and **buen mozo** (good looking). Only men are referred to as **cuadrado**—"built" or "buff."

Women can be **cuero**—"stacked" or "built."
Women can be cute—**preciosa** or **mona**, pretty—
chula, beautiful—**bella**, **hermosa**, or gorgeous—
primorosa. A beauty is **un primor**, or **una bel-
leza**. Good looking women are called, **cuerito** and
cuerazo, **buenota**, **buena curva**, **guitarra** (from
the shape of a guitar), **mango**, and alley terms
forro and **forrazo**.

Much ruder are **buen culito**, **buena percha**
and **culo chido**. Some cuter, racier adjectives are
potable, **sabrosa** (variations of tasty), **encamable**,
ensabanable (bed-able), **revolcable** ("turnable-
over"), and **mordisqueable** (toothsome, "nibble-
able").

Perita en dulce (pear in syrup) can mean a "wannabe," or chick who thinks she's gorgeous. Ugly women are called **garra, piedra** (stone) or perhaps **pellejo** (rawhide or an animal skin).

BREAD, DOUGH

Most common slang for money in border areas is **feria**, which can mean "money" or "pocket change," depending. **No traigo feria** would indicate, "I don't have any change." Further south, one hears **lana**, which literally means "wool" but probably is short for **porcelana**.

The term **plata** is understood to mean **dinero** throughout Latin America, but in Mexican border areas occasionally means **pesos** as opposed to dollars. One also hears **¿Y cuánto en inglés?** for "How much in dollars?" Another word for money is **pachucha**.

De lana means rich, so you hear odd phrases like **torta de lana** which means, not "wool sandwich," but a rich chick.

Mendigo means "beggar," but when accented on the first syllable becomes a deprecative adjective similar to "darned" or "cotton picking," or a noun similar to **cabrón**.

While **barata** is cheap, used as a noun it means a sale or bargain, as does **ganga**. Better yet would be **de balde** or **de oquis**, which mean "for free." **Abono** might be fertilizer but **en abonos** is installments or time payments (differing from **sistema de apartados**, which is "lay away") and would require an **enganche** (hook), or "down payment." A common Mexican phenomenon is **pilón**, a bonus or extra value offered in business, like an extra donut in the dozen or a free months rent.

Caifás is street slang for "pay up" and **caifás con mi lana** is "cough up now." A similar phrase is **azota mi lana** (literally, "whip me my dough"). **Chambear** means "to work," **chamba** or **jale** mean job, or gig. A salary can be called **chivo** (he-goat) or **raya** (line or scratch), while a child's weekly allowance is his **domingo.**

Droga means "debt" as well as "drug," so terms like **droguero** and **endrogado** have secondary meanings of "heavy borrower" and "debt-ridden." **Apuro** is a financial bind and "broke" can be **pelado** (peeled), **jorobado** (hunchbacked), or **brujo** (witch or sorcerer). **En la quinta** is to be in total poverty or misery, like "in the poorhouse."

GIMME A BREAK

An almost literal translation would be the expression, **Dame chanza**. Street slang uses **Al-**

iviáname to bum anything from cigarettes to favors. A similar usage is **mochate**, for mooching.

No seas gacho, carnal. Aliviáname. Mochate un frajo, would be, "Be a sport, brother. Gimme a break. Spare me a cigarette."

SHIT

Mierda is the common term and not used vulgarly as in English (where we use it for everything). **Caca** is the same in Spanish as in English, again without any other meanings. Also heard is **popó**. **Cagar** is the crude verb for shitting, **zurrar** even cruder; so **cagón** and **zurrón** both mean "shit ass" or a shitty person. **Cagadero** means "crapper."

Miar is a cruder term for peeing than **orinar** and **mingitorio** is a pisser. Piss is also **chis** or **pipí** and saying something like **Tengo que hacer pipí** is an inoffensive way of saying you want to pee. **Chorro** is crude for diarrhea and **grifo** (faucet) cruder yet.

"Bullshit" would be most politely translated as **mentiras** (lies), or perhaps the slangier **macanas** or **chucherías**. **Déjate las macanas** means, "Cut the crap." **Carambas** is used as a synonym in the since of "giving someone shit."

The term **basura** (garbage) is used more widely in Spanish and a mess, disaster, bad meal, or "piece of crap" would be a **porquería**, as would a messy house or room. One would say, **¡Ay, que cochina!**

HIP, WITH IT

Cojonudo means "ballsy," but also means, "with it," as does the old expression **muy reata** (very lariat).

Oddly, while **muy acá** (real "here") means "hip" in most of Mexico, at the border and in the U.S. one hears **muy de aquellas** (real "there") to mean "way out" or "out of this world." Any of these expressions can be inflected to mean **creido** (believer), which is the Spanish way to say somebody thinks themself to be a big deal.

TOTALLY, TO THE MAX

Remate is an auction, but has a slang sense of "all the way," so **un loco de remate**, for instance is a total nut. Another expression, **de hueso colorado** (red-boned) means dyed-in-the-wool, "totally," "last ditch," a diehard. It's often used to describe team fans or political partisans and a phrase like **Soy Mexicano de hueso colorado** is not too different from "red blooded American." Doing something "all the way out" or "full bore" is **a todo dar**, the slang version being **a todo madre**.

II. MAJOR MEXICANISMS

Tengo madre muy padre, y padre de poca madre.

Madre

This is a very complex word in Mexico and produces a major amount of rich slang. Without getting into the sociology of it, although the concept of Motherhood is held sacred in Mexico, **madre** means worthless, failed, a mess. **Una madre** is something unimportant, a put-down; **un desmadre**, is a total snafu. A **madrazo** is a heavy blow or jolt, a **madreador** or **madrino** is a bar bouncer, hit man, or goon. **Partir la madre** is to smash, destroy, or bust something. The classic Mexican insult (the equivalent of "Fuck you") is the famous **Chinga tu madre** or merely **Tu madre**.

Exceptions to all this maternal negativity are **a todo madre**, which means done right, superlative, done up brown, the whole nine yards; and **No tiene madre**—if something "has no mother" it is absolutely the coolest. However, and to illustrate the importance of context in such elemental slang, **Él no tiene madre** can also mean having no shame, so that **poca madre** is also a synonym for "jerk" (**poca abuela** avoids the crude use of the word **madre**).

Me vale madre, frequently seen on caps, shirts, and biker jackets, literally means "It makes mother to me," but is a direct equivalent to English expressions such as "I don't give a damn," or "Who gives a shit?" **Madre** used like this is considered crude speech and not acceptable in polite or mixed company, so there are euphemisms. People will say things like **"a todo M"** (like we would say, "the M word"). More transparent are such as **drema**, and the similarly scrambled **la ingada chadre**.

CHINGAR

This is another major plexus of Mexicanisms, and more complex than most non-Mexicans think.

Chingar does not mean precisely "Fuck," but comes from an older meaning of "rape" or "molest." While **No chingues con nosotros** is exactly equivalent to "Don't fuck with us," the famous **Chinga tu madre** is not sexual at all (worse, to a Mexican). **Hijo de la chingada** is "son of a bitch," but in spades. **Vete a la chingada** is rougher than "go to hell," more like "get fucked.

Hasta la quinta chingada means a long distance, "way the hell out," and can be shortened to **hasta la quinta**. A **chingazo** or **chingadazo** is a major blow or coup. **Chingadera** is a dirty trick. **Me chingaron** means "I got screwed" or "jerked around" —"they did me." **No chingues** is "lay off" or "don't fuck around."

Chingón is a compliment—a stud, the guy who can **chinga** everybody else. **Un chingo de** means a whole lot of, as in **Hace un chingo de años, Colón descubrió las Américas** (A whole heap of years ago, Columbus discovered America). The primacy of these **chinga** terms has led to a lot of expressions and ejaculations like ¡**Chin!**, ¡**Ay, Chihuahua!**, ¡**Chispas!**, ¡**Chicle!**, which are acceptable bailouts, just as we have all the "Gosh" and "Golly" words to prevent blasphemous use of "God."

Although **fregar** means cleaning or scrubbing in most Spanish countries, in Mexico it is a synonym for **chingar** in the sense of "messing with" or "bugging." **Fregado** means "snafued" or "screwed up" and **No me friegues** is "Don't bug me." A euphemism used in place of the various forms of **chingar** is **tiznar**.

LA ONDA

A constellation of sixties hippy expressions which are still quite current. **Onda** means vibrations, so **¿Que onda?** is something like, "What's the vibes?" and is the standard young, hip greeting, as ubiquitous as "What's happening?"

Buena onda, whether referring to a person or impersonal thing or event means "Good vibes." **Ella es muy buena onda** means "She's great people." Conversely, **¡Que mala onda!** means "What a bummer!" Though not as often heard, **otra onda** can mean "something else" as in "Man, that band was something else."

HUEVOS

This is another complex Mexican term. The word means "eggs," but the reference to "balls" is so strong that you have to watch out using the word at all. Polite girls would probably order **blanquillos** from a male waiter. There are a raft of egg/balls puns and jokes.

Aside from the reproductive aspects, **huevo** means "lazy" for some reason, and is reflected in a complex of vulgar expressions like **huevón** (or **huevona**) as a synonym for **flojo** or "lazy."

There's a funny poster that says, "I failed for four reasons, **La Eva, la uva, el IVA, y el huevo**." In other words, because of women ("Eve"), drink ("the grape"), taxes (the **Impuesto Valor Añadido**, or value added tax) and laziness. Though synonyms, **huevos** and **cojones** have different weights (see Chapter IV).

PUTA

Means "whore," but is more extensively used. This is what a Mexican would say if he hammered his finger. **Puta madre** is so much worse, a pretty close equivalent to the modern American use of "mother fucker." **Hijo de puta** means "bastard," "whore son," or "son of a bitch," but worse.

PEDO

Pedo means "fart," plain and simple. To say it politely would be **un ventoso** or **echar un ventoso**. But the word is used in several special ways, none polite. **Huele-pedos** (a fart-smeller) is an exact equivalent of our "brown noser" (also termed **lame-**

nalgas—a butt-licker). **No hay pedo** means "no big deal." And **bien pedo** (really fart) means "blind drunk."

CABRÓN

Is the main "bad noun," it literally means "goatish," but is used the way Americans use "ass hole" or "S. O. B." Can be fighting words, often "cleaned up" as **camión, camerón**, etc. It can be made diminutive to **cabroncito** and even **cabroncita. Un cabrón de siete suelas** (a seven-soled **cabrón**) is a "four door" or "48 carat" ass hole. Also common is **cabrón de primera** (first class). A **cabronada** is the kind of thing a **cabrón** would do.

Cabronear, even in Mexico, means to be cuckolded knowingly and **cabronismo** is to prostitute one's own wife.

PINCHE

Just as inexplicably, is the "bad adjective." Literally an assistant cook, means "nasty" and is used where Americans would say "fucking," "shitty," or what have you. "That fuckin' ass hole" would be **pinche cabrón** in Mexico.

Can be, but seldom is, used as a stand-alone adjective, **Esta comida es pinche.**

PUES

Although the dictionary meaning is "since," **pues** (and it's colloquial variations, **pos** and **pus**) are slang expressions hard to translate but frequently used. It can be used like "Well..." at the first of a sentence (**Pues, no sé** is "Well, beats me") or as we would use "then" at the end of a phrase as in, **Ándale, pues,** (Go ahead, then) or as a general emphatic, perhaps like the New York use of "yet." An obvious question or statement can be answered, **Pos, sí**.

A Tijuana **birriería** is called "**Guadalajara, Pues,**" in the way an American deli might be called,

"Brooklyn, Already."

RE-

The prefix **re-** has an augmentative effect in slang, reminiscent of the California use of "way" to mean "very." **Rebuena** is very good, **recuero** is "way stacked." **Es reloca** is "She's really nuts." Even more emphatic, less used, is **rete-**. **Te reteodio** is "I hate your guts." **Reteguapa** is "ultra super foxy." The ultimate lick is **requete-**, and **Estoy requeteseguro** is "I'm absolutely certain.

Mexicans use "super" as a similar prefix, as well. **Estaba super-enojada**, is "She was way pissed off."

EXCLAMATIONS

¡**Hijole!** is a super-Mexican expression that means things like, "Oh, wow!," "Holy cow!" or "Yikes!"

Sobres is enthusiastic agreement, like "Right on!," "Really," "You said it!" or "Yeah, let's do it!"

¡**Chale!** on the other hand, indicates disbelief as in, "Oh, sure," "No way," "Nice try" or "Tell me another one."

¡Andale! is not only "Hurry up," but also "Get with it," "Get the lead out" and can mean either "Oh, go on with you!" or "Really!" as a reply to a statement.

¡Arriba (anything)! is like "up with" or "hooray for." A Mexican recently pointed out the vast spiritual superiority of crying **¡arriba!** (up) instead of "Get down!"

¡Caramba! is famous, and can be about anything from "Wow!" to "Holy shit!" **Carambas** are also curses, hassles, and badmouthing in general.

¡Carajo! is a strong, violent oath.

¡**Mucha ropa!** (a lot of clothes), yelled at dancers or anyone in public is Spanish for "Take it off!"

¡**Caray!** is "Gosh!," "Wow!," "Holy cow!"

¡**Zaz!** or ¡**Zas!** is like "Zap!," "Pow!," "Booyah!" or "Oh, no!"

Nam Nam is "Yum Yum."

¡**Águas!** is a warning shout, like "Look out!" or "Heads!" Ghetto slang for the same thing is ¡**Trucha!** (trout) for some reason, a warning that also has tones of "Jiggers!" or "Cheese it!"

¡**Arre!** is "move it," but with a special tone since the word means "Giddyup" to a burro (hence, a dunce).

III.PEOPLE

No, **insurgente** *doesn't mean "insult people"*

GUYS

Direct Address (what you call men you're talking to):

Hombre is "Man," even as an ejaculation equivalent to "Oh, Man!" "Brother" to address a non-relative is not **hermano** but **'mano. Carnal** is like "Bro," but is likewise racially restricted except among extremely good friends. "Pal" would be **compadre**, more casually, **compa**, or at the slangiest, **compinche**. (Female equivalent, **comadre**, which has almost the sense of blacks using the term "sisters" or "sis."

Ese (literally, "that") is like "Hey, bud" and short for **ese vato**—"That guy" or "That cat," used as an attention getter like, "Hey, man," or "Hey, you."

Chico means "little one" or "kid," **joven** means "youngster," or "young man," appropriate for calling a waiter or polite inquiries of younger males. **Mijo** (contraction of **mi hijo**, "My son") is like "sonny" and is for younger boys or affectionately with friends.

Other terms for friends (**amigos, compañeros**) are **socio** (partner), **parna, cuate** (often **cuader-**

no, which really means "notebook"), **piojo** (louse), **valedor** (or **vale** for short).

Reference (referring to male third persons):

Muchacho or **chico** for young men. **Tipo** means "guy." Also very common is **chavo**. The guys are **batos** (also spelled **vatos**), **cuates, amigotes**. **Fulano** is "whoever" or "so and so" and **fulano, zutano, y mengano** are "Tom, Dick and Harry."

CHICKS

Properly **muchachas, chicas** or more formally **señoritas. Mija**, is used in direct address the same as **mijo** with males. **'Mana** is "sister" and very commonly used form of address. **Chulis** is like "cutie," "honey," or "dearie"—often used between women (or male homosexuals). **Nena**, appropriate for little girls, can also be used affectionately for younger women, something like "kiddo," "girly," or "baby." Can also be used indirectly, **¿Quién es la nena aquella? Nenorra** can also be used as both indirect reference or direct address.

Mamacita is a definite come-on type of address, used like "Hey baby," to a girl passing on the street or affectionately between lovers; also **mamasota** or **mamuchis**. **Papacito** is the male equivalent, like "Daddy" used between lovers.

Indirect terms include, **tipa**, **chava**, and **morra**, all very common and acceptable terms. **Torta** is a little sexist, but means "chick." **Ruca** means "broad" in gutter talk and is not at all polite.

Women as such are called **puris**, **murciélagas** (bats), **espátulas** and, in the alleys, **chundas**, **fisgas** and **nacas**.

LOVERS AND OTHER DETAILS

Lovers (**amantes**) and loved ones (**queridos**) are referred to as **huesos** on the street, also as **vareda**, **pato**, and **quelite**.

Affectionate and pet terms include **muñeca**, literally doll; **preciosura**, precious; **mi tesoro**, my treasure; **ricura**, richness; and **chiquitín**, teeny tiny. **Mi amor, mi vida**, and such are used towards men and women. **Viejo** is "the old man," or husband. **Papacito** or **mijo** are endearments towards men. Wives and lovers are often referred to as **vieja** ("old lady," used just like in English), or comically as **mi peor es nada**, my "better than nothing."

Girlfriends (**novias**) are referred to as **detalles** (details), **cueros** (figures), **pescados** (fish), and in the alley as **catán**.

Love affairs (**aventuras amorosas**) are **volados, aguacates, volantines**, or **movidas**.

"To flirt" is properly **coquetear**, but in Mexico is also **volarse**. While **de volada** means "suddenly," **andar de volada** also means flirting. Other terms for flirting include **dar puerta** (giving the door), **dar entrada** (giving out tickets), **pelar los dientes** (peeling the teeth), **hacer el iris** (making the iris), **mover el agua** (stirring the water), and **levantar polvo** (raising dust). "She was always flirting with the boys," could be said, **Ella levantaba polvo con los chavos**, or **Ella siempre daba entrada a los guapos.**

KIDS

There are a lot of words to use instead of **niños**. Most mean simply "small," like **chico, chiquito**, or **pequeño**. There are a lot of regional slang terms for kids, like the Mexican **chamaco**, the central American **guagua**, the Argentine **pibe**.

Babies (**infantes, bebés**) are often called **bambinos** in Mexico. Other regional slang includes **buki** (as in the famous Mexican singing group "**Los Bukis**").

Educación means "upbringing," not "education" in Spanish. **Ay, que niño más bien educado**, means "What a well brought up child."

A less well-behaved kid can be referred to as **travieso** (misbehaver) or **escuincle** (brat), **mocoso** (brat, but literally "snot nosed"). "Spoiled" is **malcriado** and **chiquiado** means "babied" or "treated like a little kid." You also hear the word **fresa** (strawberry) applied to brats, and also to dandies, like yuppie fashion plates.

Mexicans use the word **ranchero** for "shy," so one might hear **No seas rancherita** directed to a little girl hiding behind skirts.

PARENTS AND ELDERS

Parents are **padres** in Spanish; **parientes** refers to all relatives, as does **familiares**. Mexicans refer to parents as **mis jefes** (my bosses). **Jefa** is both "mother" and "old lady" in the conjugal sense, like **vieja**—you hear people say, **Juro por mi jefecita** (I swear by my old lady). Other slang words for **madre** are **mandona, venerable, sarra, margarita**. Street cant is **angustiosa** or **angustiada** (anguished).

Primo means cousin, but is also used to mean "naive"—a hick or chump.

Suegra means "mother-in-law" (with all the same jokes and bumper stickers we have), and is frequently heard as **suegrita**.

Abuela (grandmother) is almost always used in the affectionate diminutive (**abuelita**, like "granny"). Mexican kids use **Tu abuelita** in insults much like American kids use "your mama."

While one doesn't use **viejo** or **vieja** to refer to parents, **los viejos** is "the old folks."

Less kind terms for old women (**ancianas**) are **rucas, rucasianas, reliquias** (relics), **mómias** (mummies), **muñeca de antaño** (doll from yesteryear) **veteranas**. Some joking terms include the punning **Venus de mil ochocientos** (Venus from 1800), **de cuando el árbol de Noche Buena estaba en maceta** (from when the first Christmas tree was in a pot), and **cuando la Sierra Madre era señorita** (when the Sierra Madre range was unmarried).

PERSONAL CHARACTERISTICS

Many Spanish words describing people's physical and behavioral traits can be formed from root words by adding suffixes; either "**...ón**" meaning "much given to" or "**...udo**," with a sense of "characterized by." Thus words like **llorar** (cry), **boca** (mouth), or **barriga** (belly), become **llorón**—and **lloróna**, of course—(crybaby), **bocón** (bigmouth), and **barrigón** (potbellied). Similarly, **piernas** (legs), **bigotes** (mustaches), and **pelo** (hair) can transform to **piernuda** (having shapely legs), **bigotudo** (having a mustache), and **peludo** (hairy).

Remember that in Spanish most adjectives can be used as nouns so **Ella es muy piernuda** (She has great legs) and **Mira aquella peluda** (Look at that hairy chick) are equally correct usages.

Other such terms include:

comelón—a glutton or piggish
cabezón—big-headed

nalgona—woman with big butt
ojón—bug-eyed
panzón—pot-bellied
pelón—shave-headed or bald
tripón—chubby or tubby
trompudo—having big lips

Latins are quite given to calling each other by such nicknames. Any group will include people called **Gordo** (Fats), **Flaco** (Slim), **Güero** (Whitey), **Chaparro** or **Chaparrito** (Shorty), and **Chato** (Snub-nose).

Other characteristics: Curly hair is called **pelo chino** for some reason, and curls are **chinos**.

Metiche means "nosy," a "buttinsky" (from **meter** to stick in).

Hocicón from **hocico** (snout), means talkative, a "jaw jacker."

Catrín means "dude," in the sense of a dandy or "high hat." The kind of person likely to be found in places of **mucho postín**, swank, plush spots.

Comodín is a sharpie or trickster.

Gorrón means a moocher or chisler, somebody who's always putting on the bite. **Pediche** means the very same thing.

Quarrelsome people are **lión** (from **lío**, a fight), **bravero, muy pavo** (very turkey) **resalsa**, or **muy nalga** (real butt).

Ruco, meaning "old" is also seen as **racalín** in the affectionate or teasing sense.

INSULTS

We mentioned **cabrón**, the kind of word men are always calling their friends in mock insult (as well as applying in genuine insult). Next most common would be **buey**, a fairly harmless word meaning "ox." But for some reason when pronounced as **guey** or **wey** (as it often is), it becomes a harsher word, not for polite company but the kind of word with which many street types end every phrase.

Pendejo is a very Mexican expletive, a poorly defined synonym for "jerk" (but originally coming from "pubic hair") and not-acceptable in polite company. **Pendejos** are known for committing **pendejadas**. All of these words are "unisex."

Synonyms for "stupid" abound and all can be converted to the desired gender: among them are the easily recognizable **crétino, idiota, imbécil** (a "unisex" word), and **estúpido**. Be careful, this is stronger in Spanish than in English and many Mexicans, particularly women, don't like being called **estúpida** even in fun. **Tonto** (fool), **menso** (female is **mensa**, much to the chagrin of members of the IQ group), and **jetón** are a few more. **Baboso** is a good one, frequently heard, and comes from a root meaning "to drool" and is therefore a drooling idiot.

Noteworthy is the Spanish construction by which **por** is used to mean "because of" or "on account of." Playful constructions we have heard include:

Me encarcelaron por feo (they locked me up for being ugly).

Fracasé por pendejo (I failed because I was a dumb jerk).

Toma, por egoísta (take this for being selfish).
Se busca por tonto (wanted for stupidity).

IV. SEX

*You mean **culo** isn't really Spanish for "cool"?*

FUCK

Polite would be **hacer amor** or **tener relaciones sexuales**, euphemistic would be **acostar con** (go to bed with). Standard rude is **coger**, which is an exact equivalent of "to fuck" (though it really means "catch", so translate that word with extreme caution).

"A fuck" is **un cogido**. Another term is **joder**, especially in the sense of **No me jodas** (don't fuck

with me) or **jodido** (all fucked up or "snafued").
Fajar is another synonym for screw, deriving, in-
scrutably, from **fajas** (girdle or shirttail). Extremely
crude is **culear**, which also hints at sodomy.
Mexicans do not use equivalents of expressions like
"Fuck you" or "Fuck off." Another usage involves
curar, (to cure) and is used in the sense of
Cúramelo (cure me of it) or **Cúrame, mamacita**
which are sexual come-ons.

SUCK

Mamar is most like it, as in tits (mammaries,
after all) and **Mámame** means "Suck me off."
Chupar also means "to suck" and you hear **chupa**

la verga for "suck my dick." A blow job is **una chupada** or **una mamada**. **No mames**, (literally "Don't suck") means "Don't bug me" or "Lay off."

PENIS

Polite is **pene**. Crude, as in "cock" would be **la verga** (a ship's yard arm), often used as an oath or ejaculation by itself. A hard-on is called **verga dura** or a **parado** (because it "stands"). This word makes the sign on buses, **Precaución, paradas continuas**, a bit of joke).

Extremely common is **chile**, a source of many puns. **Chiludo** would mean "well hung." Among the inevitable multitude of others, some common terms

for the **partes nobles** are: **pájaro** ("bird," another
source of puns and jokes), **pito** (whistle), **pirinola**,
pinga (a general purpose word like "dick"), **picha**,
bastón (cane), **bastardo, carnada** (bait), **camote**,
perno (spike), **pistola** and **rifle** (sources of yet
more puns), **chorizo** (pork sausage), **elote**
(corncob), **hueso** (bone), **el explorador, guía
adelante** (the guide forward), and **pipí** (for a tiny
one).

Another term, **lechero** (the milkman) comes
from the Spanish use of the word **leche** (milk) to
describe semen or "cum."

VAGINA

Polite term is **vagina**. The most common crude term, equivalent to "pussy" is **panocha**, which normally means unrefined brown sugar. Another major term is **pucha**, which in Argentina means merely "drat." Others include **la cucaracha** (cockroach), **sartén** (skillet), **lunar peludo** (hairy birthmark), **nido** ("nest," for **pájaros**), **mamey, bizcocho** (biscuit), **pepita, mondongo, paparrucha**, and **concha** (sea shell).

Argolla (a washer) is a slang term for the hymen, similar to "cherry."

Traer caballo (to ride on horseback) means to menstruate as in **Ella no pudo, porque traía caballo** (She couldn't because it was her period).

TITS

The politest term is **senos**. The breast is properly called **pecho**, breasts are often called **pechitos**. "Tits" is most directly equivalent to **chichis** or **chichornias**, and a busty woman is a **chichona**. Mexico City slang is **repisas** (shelves). Other terms are **chimeneas** (chimneys), **peras** (pears), **agarraderas** (subway hand straps), **alimentos** (food, nourishment), **defensas** (bumpers), or **educación** (as in **Ella tuvo una buena educación**.)

ASS

Mexicans call the butt **las nalgas** (buttocks), or the slangier **nachas**. A cutsier term like "booty," more used by women, is **pompis**. "Tail" is **cola**. The anus is **ano**, asshole is **coño**; both are more popularly expressed as **culo**. The anus is also referred to as **el chico, el polo sur** (the South Pole), and **ojete**, commonly written phonetically as **OGT**.

Mexicans don't call people "ass holes" like we do, although one hears **culero**, which has a sense of "coward" about it, one who shows his anus when running away.

Obviously the many English expressions like "kick ass," "I'm after your ass," "piece of ass," etc. don't translate.

A spanking is a **nalgada**. **Trasero** means "rear end" or "butt" and a shapely female behind is often called **diferencial** (a car's rear end). The term **mapa mundi** (world map) is used to mean a view of the *derriere*, somewhat similar to the English slang, "moon."

A cute expression for **culo** is **cucu**, and a popular party song is "**No Te Metas Con Mi Cucu**." Good for laughs is to convert the lyric to **mi rucu**, which subtly adds the concept of **ruco** or "old."

BALLS

In addition to the ubiquitous **huevos**, the gonads, properly **criadillas** or **testículos**, are called **cojones, cuates, óvalos, bolas**, or in alley talk, **obstáculos**.

Cojones is most often used as "balls" in the sense of bravery or brashness and **tener cojones** (like **tener tripas**) means "having guts." **Cojonudo** is "ballsy" and a hell of a fellow.

DOING IT

Though of limited utility, these expressions for "getting it on" are so colorful we knew you'd want to know them: **bastardear, echar un palo** (throw the stick), **medir su aceite** (check her oil), **darle a comer al chango** (feed the monkey), **revisar los interiores** (redecorate the interior), **subir al guayabo** (climb the guava tree), **andar por caderas** (walk on the hips), **mojar el barbón** (wet the bearded one), **tomar medidas por dentro** (take inside measurements), **tronar los huesitos** (rattle the bones), **aplicar inyección intrapiernosa** (give an intra-leg injection), **reunir los ombligos** (join bellybuttons).

Two cutsie expressions for "making it" are the **cuchi-cuchi** or **riqui-riqui**. More local color: to deflower a woman is **hacer un favor** (do a favor),

tronar el parche (blow the patch), **romper el tambor** (rip the drum), **dejar sin cosita**, and **descorchar** (uncork).

MASTURBATION

For men, often involves variations on **puño** (fist). Hence **puñetazo** and **hacer la puñeta** (making like a pump shotgun). One also hears **paja** (straw) and **hacer paja** to mean "jacking off." A **puñetero** or **pajero** is therefore a chronic masturbator or jackoff. Female self-service (and finger-fucking in general) is **dedear** (fingering).

HEAVY PETTING

When caresses (**caricias**) and hugs (**abrazos**) get specific they are called other things. **Sobas** are hugs, but **sobar** also applies to all degrees of petting. **Apapachar**, for instance is to "cop a feel" and **chichonear** means to fondle the breasts. **Dedear** is to finger whatever parts with an eye to **cachondear** (sexually excite).

A person thus made **cachondo** has **ansias** or "the hots." Another term is **soplar**, in this sense meaning to get hot, usually said of women. Someone with chronic "hots" is said to be **caliente**.

Empelotado means both naked and madly in love or moonstruck (which could also be said **locamente enamorado** or **encadicalo**). Naked is also **desnuda** or **encuerado**. **Encuérate** means "get naked." **Hazme piojito** (make me a louse) means "Scratch me on the head."

PREGNANT

Unfortunately (though sometimes appropriately, no doubt) **embarazada** is the word for both "pregnant" and "embarrassed." This can be clarified by using **encinta** or **esperando un bebé** for the first case and **pena** or **me da pena** for "embarrassment" or "he embarrassed me." **Coneja** is a woman who is always "knocked up." There is further confusion since **aborto** means both "abortion" and "miscarriage" though **abortaje** is always the former. Abortionists are called **espantacigüenas** (scare-storks) or, extremely crudely, **cuchareros**. Childbirth is a **parto**, by the way, and a midwife or obstetrician is a **partera**.

HOMOSEXUAL

Among the inevitable swarm of words and innuendo the polite or correct term is **homosexual**. A light, joking term similar to "fairy" or "flit" is **lilo**. The "standard" term, not completely polite but acceptable, is **joto**. A harsh term, comparable to "faggot" would be **puto** (masc. of **puta**, whore). **Putón** is a flaming faggot. Many Americans know **maricón**, (or **marica**, the same word) which can be used as a synonym for gay, but actually means "sissy" or "effeminate."

The female equivalent, like "butch," would be **marimacha**. With women, the correct term would be **lesbiana**. The word "gay" is used in Mexico, though the pronunciation is often "Spanished" to sound like the English word "guy." Both male and female homosexuality are "41," or **cuarenta y uno**. Reason is unsure, but possibly because it is the reverse of 14 or **catorce**, which means "sex" or "fuck." Incidentally, in Spanish countries AIDS is **el SIDA** and those with AIDS are **sidosos**.

KINKY

This word doesn't have many Spanish equivalents other than prosaic ones like **pervertido** or **aberraciones sexuales**. Most terms like **invertido** and **volteado** (turned over) refer to homosexuality and most English technical terms transliterate (**masoquismo, sadismo, fetichismo**, etc.), However the expression **de los otros** ("of the others") denotes deviation and **aves raros** can also refer to the kinky.

PROMISCUITY

As in English, there is a wide range of judgmental terms for female promiscuity. In between

juilona (a loose, gadabout girl) and **puta** (an outright whore), are **coscolina** (slut) and **piruja** (a "pro/am" slut), while **resbalosa** is a tease. **Sarrastra** is a woman of worst possible morals and reputation.

Amasia is a kept woman or mistress (and can also be **amasio**) and **amasiato** is a common-law mate.

On the male side of the ledger, **mujeriego** or **mujereo** is a womanizer (the female equivalent would be **hombreriega**. **Birriondo** means a stud or cocksman, **chichonero** is a "tit man" and **garañón** is an animal at stud, and thus a loose male or wolf, though the normal Mexican term for "wolf" is

tiburón (shark). A **congalero** (from **congal**—bordello) is a whore-hopper or sexual low life.

Lower yet is to **gatear**—household servant girls, generally from low, uneducated classes, are called **gatas** (cats) and to pursue them sexually is to **gatear** which means "crawl" in different context.

THE DEMIMONDE

For purely sociological reasons, we present a list of terms used in "red light" areas:

Condom: Simple safety requires a knowledge of technical terminology. "Rubbers" are properly called **condón**, or **preservativo** (a telling word in this

day and age), they are also known as **diablito,
portalápiz** (pencil box), **Doña Prudencia,
sombrero de Panamá, paraguas** (umbrella), **im-
permeable** (raincoat), **globito** or **bomba** (both
words meaning balloon), **caperucita en carnada**
(caped bait), or **desafinador** ("untuner").

Prostitute: Formally **prostituta**, often shortened to **prosti**, a whore is called a **puta**. There are
many other terms, like **lionas**, (quarrelsome),
araña (spider), **gallina** (hen), **ratera**. A street-
walker is a **callejera**, a pushy one is a **garrapata**
("grabs-your-paw"), and an ugly one, a **gaviota** (sea
gull).

Brothel: There are a lot of prudish terms like **casa non sancta, casa de citas, casa de mala nota**, but a **burdel** is usually called **congal** and some street terms are **bodio, zumbido, cortijo, manflota**, and **bule.**

"B Girls:" Terms for **cabareteras** include the common **fichera** (girls who are paid for tokens or **fichas** they get for drinks sold at their tables), **linas, peseras , ratoneras, exprimidoras**. They could also be exotic dancers (**bailarinas**), of course, or strippers (**vedéttes**—pronounced in French style— or **encueratrices**).

Madame: **Madre Superiora, madrina, madrota, doña de las naguas** (lady of the petticoats), **abadesa** (abbess), or **jefa de relaciones públicas** (head of public relations).

Pimp: Properly **tratante de blancas** (trader in white women), they are also called **padrote, cinturita**, or **fundillero** (the latter from **fundillo**, the anus). "Procurer" is also **alcahuete** and, for that matter **alcahueta**.

GENERAL SEX PISTOLS

The word **sexy** is used in Mexico. Horny is most usually **jadeoso**, literally "panting." A "quickie" is **un rapidín**, and a "nooner" is the Spanish word for matinee, **tardeada**. Mexicans also use "come" in the sexual sense and **venirse juntos** means to come together in both senses. In the reflexive, **venir** almost always means to climax: **Me vine** means "I came." Another way to say it would be **Me gocé** (I enjoyed myself). There is a phrase **el mismo orgasmo**, which means "the most," "the main event."

Cute for panties is **chones** and, even cuter, **choninos**.

"Crabs," or lice are **piojos, chatos,** or **ladillas.**

Mexicans are very big on the concept of "horns," of being cuckolded. To **poner cuernos** (put horns) on someone is to have carnal knowledge of his wife. (Reverse "horning" is not mentioned or at least not

named.) A cuckold is a **cornudo**. (And would joking-
ly be called "**Cornelio**.")

"**Sancho**" is an interesting character, the per-
sonification of the man who comes in and puts horns
on hubby while he's away. There are songs about
Sancho (and also **Sancha**).

V. DRUGS

Just say, "¡No way, José!"

MARIJUANA

Mota means "pot," the main word used in most places, with **yerba** or **hierba** (herb) a close second. But as in English, there are many colorful terms. Some are just puns on **mota**, like **motocicleta** or **motivosa**. Others are nicknames and brand names like **clorofila**, **grifa**, **de la verde**, **de la buena**, or **fina esmeralda**. Unlikely to be heard by an outsider, but sufficiently colorful to be shared, are: **coliflor tostada** (toasted cauliflower), **orégano**

chino (chinese oregano), **zacate inglés** (English hay), **doradilla** (little golden), **doña diabla** (devil lady), **dama de la ardiente cabellera** (lady of the horny hairdo), **nalga de ángel** (angel's butt), **trueno verde** (green thunder), and **motor de chorro** (jet engine).

Mexican "heads" (**marihuanos**) say **quemar** (burning) or **tostar** (toasting) instead of smoking. Other terms include, **motorizar** ("motorize," but a pun on **mota**), **dorar** (gild or toast golden brown), **enyerbar** ("to herb"), **grifear,** and the poetic **enamoriscar**, a hybrid of **enamorar** (to fall in love) and **mordisquear** (to nibble).

A "hit" or "toke" is an **acelerón**. Unlike our colorful selection of words for "joint," Spanish mostly sticks with **cigarro** and (although there is the street term **porro**) the roach or butt is **bachicha**.

An interesting etymology here: "Your turn" in Spanish would be **Te toca** or **Tu toque**. Start passing one around in Mexico and it suddenly becomes clear where a silly word like "toke" came from. It's just how one tokes over the line.

ALCOHOL

See "Party Time," Section VII.

CIGARETTES

Frajo is common street slang, especially in the North. **Chilango** street slang is **menurrón**. One also hears **cartucho** or **tambillo**. Old timers still say **un chiva**. A cute local equivalent for "coffin nails" is **tacos de cáncer**.

OTHERS

Cocaine (**cocaína**) is called **coca** on the street, oddly also what you ask for when ordering a Coca-Cola. Presumably confusion will be minimal. Heroin (**heroína**) is called **chiva** by traffickers (**traficantes**, **narcos** or **drogueros**).

Other terms for opiates include, **nieve** (snow), **cura** (meaning both "priest" and "cure"), **tecata**, **medicina**, **doña blanca** (white lady). Opium and brown heroin from Mexico are sometimes called **chicloso de mandarín** (Mandarin chewing gum), **chocolate chino** (chinese chocolate) or, more commonly, **Chinaloa** (Sinaloa being a major producing state).

Around the border, one is occasionally offered **Sherm**, which is PCP in case you'd like to avoid that experience.

You're probably expecting all sorts of warnings and disclaimers about drugs, so why should we bother? Suffice it to say that an acquaintanceship with drugs in Mexico or Latin American can quickly put one on a first name basis with The Law, so here are some helpful terms to while away the time.

CRIME AND PUNISHMENT

Cops

The **policía** or **patrulla** are most often called **placas** (badges) on the streets instead of **oficial**. An underground **Chilango** term is **garfil**.

There are also many terms like **azul, tamarindo, jaiba, chocolate, chocomilk** that derive from uniform color and some terms for traffic cops (like **lobo** or **feroz**) that derive from the natural Mexican hatred for the cops that hit them up for the **mordida** on the road. A cop much given to the "take" is a **mordelón**.

Being arrested (**aprehendido, arrestado, detenido**) is called by verbs like **agarrar** (grab), **torcer** (twist), **rodar** (roll), and the alley-wise **aparuscar** or **amacizar**. Or simply, **Me preguntaron, pero no me invitaron,** (They questioned me, but didn't "invite" me.) The "paddy wagon" is **júlia**.

Jail and prison

Terms for jail (**cárcel**, **calabozo**) or prison
(**penitenciaría**, **prisión**) are many. Jail is often
called the **tambo** or **bote** and a very common street
term for prison (or **la peni**) is **la pinta**, derived from
the expression **hacer pinta** (to play hookey from
school).

Stealing

Street terms for **robar** include **borrar** (erase),
bajar (lower), **pegar** (hit), **cleptomanear**, **pelar**
(peel), **carrancear**, **birlar** and **trabajar con fé**

(work with faith—applied to burglarizing). Thieves, properly **ladrones** or **rateros** are called **uñas** (fingernails) or **ratones** (rats) on the street.

To "squeal" is **soplar** (blow) and a "snitch" is a **rata** or **soplón**. To snitch someone off is to **poner rata** or **poner dedo**.

VI. ROCK AND ROLL

¿Queremos qué?

Actually, most hip Mexican rock slang is merely English. You won't need translations to speak of "punk," "heavy metal," "rap," "jazz," "blues," "country" or "rock" music. Those wishing to explore Mexican music might ask about **ranchero** or **norteño** (cowboy, country music), **cúmbia** or **música tropical** (infectious Caribbean boogie music), **baladas** ("vocal" music), or **bailables** (dance music).

Disco is both a record and a discotheque, a **discoteca** is a record store. "Hits" are **éxitos** or **pegaditos** hit music is **música de mucho pegue**. To play music in Spanish is **tocar**.

Along with **música rock**, there are words like **rocanrolero** (a rocker, as in the Timbiriche hit, **El Gato Rocanrolero**) and **roquear** meaning to rock, as in the expression **roqueándote toda la noche** (rocking you all night long). An expression almost sure to get a laugh is **"¡Queremos rock!"** (We want rock), a tag line of a famous television comedian.

While **cine** is "the movies," by the way, "film" is **película** and **de película** means "fabulous," like something out of a movie. **Toda la película** (the whole movie), on the other hand, means "the whole nine yards," "the whole song and dance," "the works."

VII. PARTY TIME

You mean **birria** *really* <u>is</u> *Spanish for "beer"?*

PARTY

    Fiestas are parties, all right, but the term more often used for partying down is **pachanga**, and "to party" is **pachanguear**. **Pachanguero** is like "party hearty" or "party animal" and "party doll" or "party girl" would be **nena pachanguera**. Also used are **reventón** (literally, a "blowout") or **reve** for short. A **parranda** or **francachela** is a drunken spree or orgy, **tertulia** a dance party, and **frasca** or

fracas an impromptu bash. A special Hispanic fancy is the **lunada**, a moonlight beach party.

A **borrachera** is a drunken bash, and when combined with **boda** (wedding) yields the popular pun "**bodachera**" to mean a very wet wedding. **Vacilón** means "having a ball," "feeling no pain."

EATING

Slang terms for **comer** include: **filiar**, very big in the capital, and **empacar** (pack).

Ways of saying, "Tie on the feed bag" include: **menear la quijada** (wiggle the jaw), **mover el bigote** (move the mustache). **Hambre** (hunger) can also be **ambrosia, filo** or **filomeno**. "I'm hungry," is **Tengo ambrosia** on the streets.

One hears **tortillas** called **gordas, guarnelas, guarnetas, sorias, discos** and, among the with-it, **long pleis**. Instead of **frijoles**, beans are sometimes called **balas, balines, parque, los completadores, chispolitos,** or the street word, **parraleños**.

DRINKING

While the verb "to drink" is technically **beber**, most people have learned that everyone really says **tomar**. The waiter asks, **¿Algo de tomar?**, for

"Anything to drink?" and the cop asks **¿Estabas tomando?** (You been drinking?).

A drink, as in "Lets have a drink," is **un trago** from **tragar,** to swallow or gulp. Drinks are also referred to as **copas,** technically stemmed glasses. Oddly, while **jalón** (a pull) means a "snort," **empujar** (push) means to drink steadily. "Shots" or "belts" of booze are also termed **farolazos** (beams from searchlights) and **fajos** (fistfuls).

Slangier words for imbibing are **infle, libar,** and **chupar.** The latter is quite common and means "suck," so **Vamos a chupar unas chelas** means "Let's go suck some suds." You could also say, **Vamos**

al pomo, pomo meaning a bottle or drink. Very slangy are such words as **piular**, or **gargarear** (gargle).

Bautizar (baptize) means to water down a drink and a **piquete** (sting) is a shot "spiked" into a drink. **Raspabuche** ("scrape-throat") is rot-gut liquor. **Disparar** (to shoot or fire a round) means to spring for the drinks, pick up the tab, buy the round.

A bit of drinking folklore in Mexico, by the way, is that one never orders a "last" drink—the "one for the road" is **la penúltima** or, as in the old movies, **la del estribo**, literally "one for the running board" or "one for the stirrup." It's worth noting, by the way, that in Mexico especially, a **cantina** is a bar for men only. You see "Ladies' Bars" that admit both sexes.

BEER

Cheve, **chevecha**, and **chela** are slang for **cerveza** like "suds" or "brewski." One also hears **serpentina** and in the North one hears **birria**, (actually a goat stew) for "beer," a joking "Spanishization" of American pronunciation. In Guadalajara there are T-shirts that say **Cheves, Chavas, y Chivas**—Beers, chicks, and the famous Chivas soccer team.

DRUNK

Borracho is the common term, directly equivalent, although **ebrio** is more proper and **briago** is heard. **Borrachón** is a drunk, souse, or just somebody who gets drunk a lot. **Emborrachar** means to get drunk. In Mexico, as the saying goes, **Más vale ser un borracho conocido que un Alcohólico Anónimo**, better a well-known drunk than an anonymous alcoholic.

Teporocho also means drunk. **Alumbrado** and **alumbrarse** are, literally, "lit" and "to get lit" and **encandilado** means the same—lit up like a Christmas tree. **Enchispado** (sparky) is a happy drunk and a **cohete** (skyrocket) is a guy who is "blasted." You also hear **ahogado** (drowned) and **al color** (stewed) for "bombed." **Bien pedo** means "really smashed," but is a crude term, since **pedo** means "fart."

The Spanish term for "hangover," should you get that far, is one of the most picturesque in the language—**la cruda**. No wonder it eclipses the proper term, **la resaca**. Next time you crude out, try to remember the Mexican proverb, **Evite la cruda, permanezca borracho**. (Avoid hangovers, stay drunk). "Sober" and "sobriety," for those interested, are **"sobrio"** and **"la sobriedad."**

GAMES AND SPORTS

Other than **dominos**, party and bar games generally use dice **(dados)** in games like **cubilete** (with a throwing cup) and **chingona** (with poker dice), or cards (formally **naipes**, but **gatas** in the jailhouse and streets).

A deck of cards is a **baraja** and **barajar** is to shuffle the deck. There are different games and even decks in Mexico, but you can find games of spades and poker (cribbage is unknown, alas). Poker terminology is strange, though. Aces are **ases** and kings **reyes** as expected, but queens are **cüinas** and jacks, **jotas** (the letter "j"). Four of a kind is a **poker** and full house is **a ful** (rhymes with "fool"). You play for **fichas** (chips).

You don't find darts in Mexico, but there are **billares** (pool or billiards) and you might find a **boliche** (bowling alley).

When watching sports you will find a proliferation of English terms, even in soccer (which most people know is called **fútbol**). You hear of the **futbolistas** making a **gol**, or being **ofsayd** (offside)—and this is more so in other sports such as **básquetbol**, **box**, **volibol** and **fútbol americano**. One hears of **jonrons** (home runs), **noqueos** (knockouts), and **cachas** (catches). You even hear the ball called **bola**, instead of **pelota**.

There are universal terms like **equipo** (team),
empate (a tie), **campeonato** (championship), and
temporada (season), of course. But plays and
strategies use a morass of terms that can take years
to learn, so it's also usually easier to use English
terms for American sports, rather than try to learn
complicated Spanish translations like **medio jar-
dinero** (middle gardener) for "center fielder" or
mariscal de campo (field marshall) for "quarter-
back."

VIII. NICKNAMES OF ORIGIN

*Is a **gringo** worse than a **chilango**?*

There is a lot of slang directed at geographical origins. Americans are often politely called **americanos**, but there are those who insist that since "America" is two big continents, Americans should refer to themselves as **norteamericanos** or the ridiculously unutterable **estadounidenses**. (It should be pointed out that both Canadians and Mexicans are also North Americans and that Mexico is formally "The United States of Mexico.") This makes the familiar term **gringo** seem attractive, but it could be noted that it is a bit of a slur and might embarrass or amuse many Mexicans, like a black calling himself or allowing himself to be called a "boogie" or "sambo." A good middle ground is **gabacho**, which is applied almost exclusively to Americans, though it originally meant "Frenchman." The current slang for the French is **franchutes**.

Many Mexican regions have colorful slang terms for their natives, nicknames generally as inexplicable as "Tar heels," "Jay hawkers," and "Knickerbockers." The most common of these is **chilango**, a native of Mexico City or the surrounding Distrito Federal. **Chilangos** use the term proudly, but to others it has varying degrees of deprecation, worse even than "New Yorker" in the states. For instance, there are highway graffiti that say, **"Haz patria, mata a un chilango"**—essentially, "Be patriotic, kill a Chilango." You hear Mexico City and the D.F. called **Chilangolandia** (and the U.S. called **Gringolandia**.)

Another classic appellation is **tapatío**, a native of Guadalajara. A term of extreme pride and without the negative feel of **chilango**, **tapatío** things are very Mexican. **Ojos tapatíos** is a famous song about the distinctive European eyes of **tapatías**, and the real name for the famous "Mexican Hat Dance" is **"Jarabe Tapatío."**

People from Monterrey are called **regiomon-tanos** and have a reputation for being cheapskates, like our jokes stereotyping Scotsmen or Jews as "tight," but less good natured. In Mexico, by the way, "tightwad" is **codo** (elbow) and can be signified by tapping the elbow.

Other regional nicknames include:
culiche—From Culiacán, in Sinaloa
hidrocálidos—Aguascalientes
jarochos—Veracruz
jalisquillos—State of Jalisco (a slight slur)
abajeños—The lower (or **abajo**) part of Jalisco
tijuas—Tijuana
choyeros—Ciudad Constitución, B.C.

cachanilla—Baja California, specifically, Mexicali
boxito or **boshito**—the Yucatán peninsula
arascos—Michoacán
campechano—Campeche
alacrán(scorpion)—Durango
jaibo—Tampico
borinqueño—Puerto Rico
gachupín—Spain
chale—China or South East Asia
tejano—Texas

IX. BORDER SLANG

Spanglish, **inglesito,** *and* **cholismos**

Border jargon doesn't just derive from the blending that infuriates purists on both sides; it has it's own founts of new expressions, many from the **barrios** of Tijuana and Los Angeles (or, as the **Pachucos** would say it, "**Los**"). Here's a quick glimpse at this complex web of language.

Cholos are variously L.A. street punks, Mexican American gangsters, or (according to Mexicans) any sort of low rider low-lifes that come south of the border. Though the word is ill-defined, there is a definite **Cholo** style, though it might change. **Cholos** are the cultural descendants of the **Pachucos** (or **Chucos**), who in turn followed the zoot suit Latinos of the 1950's. Much of the border lingo is their invention, although much is also coined by recent immigrants struggling with the language.

The most notable phrase in **Cholo** Spanish is "**Ese**" (that) as an address or referring to someone. Also famous are **"Ahí te huacho"** (I'll "watch" you here—I'll see you later) which is frequently stylized even more to **"Ayte guacho."** The **Cholo caló** is characterized by phrases like **sácala** (take it out) for "spare me some dope," **tirar la vuelta** (throw the corner) for "to die," **nuestro barrio rifa sin zafos** (our neighborhood fights all the time).

Some words are merely slurred Spanish, like **"Quiubo"** from **¿Qué hubo?** to mean "What's with you?" Some are twisted down from English like a customized motorcycle; **biklas** (bikes, motorbikes) for instance, or **chopear** for "chopping" a car, **blofear** for bluffing at poker, or grabbed straight out of English like **los babidols**.

Others are complex puns and jokes, with syllables added on over the years until they emerge as enigmas like the famous **nariz boleada** (polished nose) to mean simply **nada**. At it's best, the border slang is free-wheeling and spontaneously creative: There is little theory behind a sign that says, **Se fixean flats** or a waitress calling for **crema de whip**.

A short glossary:

agringarse—to become "gringofied," to adopt Northern ways.
andar lurias—to be crazy, "off the rocker"
chafa—cheap, low class, "Made in Taiwan"
echarnos unas birrias—to drink (toss ourselves) some beers
gabardinos—Americans (play on **gabacho**)
jura—cops

grifo—stoned on marijuana
el mono—the movies
buti—**mucho**, a lot
loro—(parrot), friend, **amigo**
pacha—bottle, therefore "booze"
pinero—chatterbox, talkative
pielas—beers
picha—to invite
cofiro—coffee
a pincél—(artist's paintbrush) on foot, walking
tirar bronca—to raise a "beef," to "bitch" at someone
masticar totacha—speak (or "chew") English
no hay piri—don't worry, don't sweat it
borlo—a party

cantonear—reside (from **cantón**, house)
de bolón, pin-pon—quickly, chop-chop
tripear por burra—take a trip on a bus
clavado—(nailed) in love, having a "crush"
clavarse—read something or hear it on TV
dompear—to dump
guara—water
raite—a ride, a lift (this is spreading throughout Mexico and is hip among young people in the capital)
bobos—lazy
bonche—bunch
lonche—lunch (in Mexico, one sees **loncherías** and a **lonche** is often a submarine sandwich)
broder—brother

cachar—to catch, or a baseball catcher; this is catching on in Mexico, since **coger** (to catch) also means "to fuck" and is awkward to use

chavalo—a kid

checar—to check up, **cheques** to mean checks is now common in Mexico

donas—donuts

escuadra—a carpenter's square, therefore a "square" or "nerd"

huira—a young girl, chick

hayna—a broad, babe, honey

jale—a job or "gig"

monis—American money

lisa—(smooth) shirt

pai—pie: **pai de queso** is cheese cake

piquiniqui—picnic
panqueque—pancakes, or even pound cake
saina—a sign, like **saina de neón**

X. SOME BASICS

Now You Tell Us

GREETINGS AND GOODBYES

Apart from the usual and **¿Qué onda?**, **¿Qué transas?** is a hip way to ask what's up or to imply "What's the deal?" (transaction). **Bien transa**, on the other hand means someone is a cheat. Recently you hear **¿Cómo estamos?** as a greeting. This "How are we doing?" has a friendly ring and is good for the beginner who can't sort out which second person form he wants to use.

Popular ways to say "See you later" are **nos vemos** (we'll see each other) or just **luego** (later), with **al rato** (in a little while) for short-term separations. More formally, one usually hears **Que te vaya bien** (fare you well). **Baybay** (pronounced "bye-bye") is considered hip in Mexico, just as we use "**ciao**," which is also used in Latin America and particularly the heavily Italian Argentina, where it is spelled "**chiau**."

YES, NO, AND TO WHOM

Sí

Simón, is, sábanas, cilindros, sifón, cigarros, and the **pochismo** or "Spanglish" expression,

"**Claro que *yes*,**" (a common expression, used in the same spirit that we would say "Who, *moi*?") **Claro** is, of course, the way Spanish speakers say, "Of course," and slangsters often express "sure," "you bet," etc. as **clarón**, or **clarinete**.

No

Nel is popular, especially on the street, and as a sassy response like "Nope" or "Nah," you also hear **Nel pastel**, and **Nones cantones**.

Nada or no hay

Big concepts in Mexico—**No hay, no hay** is a TV catch phrase seen on bumper stickers and decals (**calcomanías** in Spanish) and often good for a laugh.

Other forms of "no got" are **nadaza, onia, nenél, nanay, ni fu, ni sopa, ni zócalo, ni marta, Negrete, Nicanor, Nicolás**, (and the Spanishized **inglesito** *"never in* **mai cochin laif"**).

Ni jota and other **"ni"** expressions are often used to mean you didn't understand something. If someone says, "¿**Entiendes?**" a response of "**Ni Marta**" means "Not a word." **Ni sueños** is a come-back to keep in mind, by the way—it means "Not in your wildest dreams."

Yo

Even a simple word like "I" gets slanged. **Melón, menta, me manta, Yolanda**, and the **caló** gutter slang, **mendurria** are heard.

Tú, usted

Instead of **tú** or **ti**, slangsters often use words like **tunas, tiburcio**, and the **caló** expression **mendorasqui** for "you."

It can quickly be seen here that one can improvise synonyms for **sí, no, mi** and other stock responses by playing with words that start with the same syllable.

FEATURES AND PHYSICAL PROPERTIES

The Human Face

Just as we use words like "mug" and "map," Spanish has slang terms for the face, many stemming from the **caló** term, **fila**. They include: **filharmónica, catequismo, la feroz** (the ferocious), and **fachada** ("facade," **"Es pura facha"** means, "He's all front" or "all bluff;" **desfachatez** is "sassy").

The Human Head

Called variously **coco** (coconut), **adobe**, **maceta** (flower pot), **azotea** (a flat roof), **calabaza** (squash, calabash), **chiluca, choya,** and **chayote.**

Eyes are sometimes called **candorros, linternas, oclayos** or **ventanas** instead of **ojos.** Caló for "see" or "look at" replaces **ver, mirar** or **observar** with **mirujear, riflear,** or **clachar.**

The Body

La pata means "paw" or foot of an animal, but is used humorously. **Meter la pata** means "to put your foot in it" (as in your mouth). **Que mala pata** means

"What a bum break," especially in South America. **Estirar la pata** (stretch out the foot), means "to kick the bucket." **Patas arriba** means "upside down," but in a folksy way like, "end over teakettle."

MISCELLANEOUS

achichincle a "brown noser"
alzado snooty, stuck-up
bembo a jerk, a bimbo
berrinche a tantrum **berrinchudo** means pouting or given to childish fits
bobo an idiot or dunce. It was popular to refer to the Mexican soap opera **Cuna de Lobos** (Cradle of Wolves) as **Cuna de Bobos.**
bruto coarse, uncouth, stupid, a redneck

bicho a bug or any tiny animal, an insignificant person, used chidingly like "twerp" or "knucklehead"

burra, veloz bicycle

bola a street brawl, a "rumble"

cabula pesado, a jerk or creep (adjective or noun)

camellar (to "camel") to walk or stroll, at the border, means to work, especially in the field

carterista a pickpocket

chabacano cheap, vulgar, common

chévere cool, hip, especially in Central America

chiflado crazy, loony, **loco**

chinche (bedbug) a pest, obnoxious person

piropo compliment, but to give lavish compliments to the opposite sex is **echar flores** (throw flowers)

conchudo (having a shell) a cynic, a "hard case"
corriente cheap, vulgar, common (said of people,
or language)
cucaracha a jalopy or "beater" also **carrucha**
dar color (to give color) street talk for knowing or
recognizing someone, **No te doy color** is "I don't
know you from Adam."
dengue prude, sissy, prissy
espantajo (scarecrow) a weirdo or "freak"
feón an ugly sucker **medio feón** (or **media feona**
is "about half ugly"
güero refers to light hair or skin, thus can mean
"fair," "Whitey," "Blondie." In Mexico often used as
a synonym for gringo.
cantón house, is common street talk, but widely
understood; also **cantera, cuartel, chantel** or

jaula (cage); **gan** or **chachimba** are gutter slang.
changuita (little monkey) your "squeeze," the girl
you are making it with at the moment
fusca a pistol
grueso a punk, "greaseball," street scum, "biker"
jalonero or **jaladar** good company, a cool person
to hang out with
¡lagarto! (lizard) is a cry to take away bad luck
lagartitos are pushups
lata (tin can) a hassle, bother, pain in the butt
lépero (leper) a foul-mouthed, obscene creep, a
"gross-out artist"
ligue (from **ligar**, to tie up) means a sexual or
romantic conquest (or **conquista**, as they say)
lucha libre wrestling, especially professional style
llanta (tire) belly or "spare tire" of fat

mamón or **mamey** a jerk, a pain in the ass
mandilón (from **mandil**—apron) hen-pecked or
"apron-stringed"
muy gente ("very people") great folks, salt of the
Earth, jolly good fellow
naco a nerd or hick, low class oaf
palanca (lever) pull, clout. **"Tiene palanca con
el ayuntamiento"** means "He's got pull at City
Hall"
paparrucha a fib or "white lie"
pissed off— **enojado** can be "slangized" to **en-
cabronado**, or phrases like **Me choca** or **Me
crispa** indicate that something tees one off.
chocante is "obnoxious," a piss-off
pichón (pigeon) a "sucker," "chump," or "mark"
gusano (worm) railroad

ranfla border slang for a custom rod or "low rider"
¡saco! said when breaking wind
li is common for **calle**, street. Also **calletana,
lleca,** and **fiusa**
tianguis swap meet, flea market
tijera (scissors) a tattle tale, a fink
tilico "wasted," starved, a walking skeleton
tocayo namesake, person (or saint) with same
name
trompillo "the raspberry," farting sound with lips
quedada (one left or ignored) a wallflower
zafado crazy, **loco**
zonzo a moron, a gooner

English Index

Photocopy this handy ORDER FORM
Other books available from In One EAR Publications:
_____**Spanish Lingo for the Savvy Gringo** ($12.95)
_____**Bilingual Cooking** ($12.95)
_____**Bilingual Recipes** ($4.95)
_____**Mexican Slang: A guide** ($6.95)
Write for free catalog of *friendly foreign language learning*!
Mark quantity of each book you want. Add local sales tax and
$2.00 postage and handling per book. Please send book(s) to:

name_____
address_____
city, state, zip_____
Make check or money order payable to: In One Ear.
Mail your order to:
In One EAR Publications
29481 Manzanita Drive
Campo CA 91906-1128
Wholesale discounts available, inquiries welcome.
Credit card orders, call toll-free **1-(800) 356-9315**